AI Personal Tax Optimization

How Artificial Intelligence Helps You Keep More of What You Earn

By Joe Correa

Published by Live Stronger Faster

This book is for educational and informational purposes only. The author and publisher are not engaged in rendering legal, financial, tax, or other professional advice. Readers should consult a qualified professional before making any financial decisions.

First Edition

Table of Contents

Introduction 5

Chapter 1: The Digital Tax Revolution 11

Chapter 2: The Rise of the Fully Automated Tax System 18

Chapter 3: Real-Time Tax Intelligence 24

Chapter 4: Life Inside a Zero-Stress Tax System 29

Chapter 5: Trust, Transparency, and the New Relationship With Taxes 35

Chapter 6: AI as Your Personal Tax Co-Pilot 42

Chapter 7: Preparing for a World of Invisible Taxes 49

Chapter 8: Designing a Life Around Effortless Compliance 58

Chapter 9: Financial Freedom in an AI-Managed World 66

Chapter 10: The End of Tax Anxiety and the Beginning of Financial Peace 74

Final Thoughts 82

Introduction

The future of personal taxes is arriving faster than anyone expected, and it is not simply an upgrade to the old system but a complete reinvention of how money, income, reporting, and compliance work in the digital age. For more than a century, taxpayers have been trapped in a manual, stressful, error-prone process that forces people to decode complex laws, gather mountains of documents, and hope that nothing is wrong after they submit their returns. Artificial intelligence is now dissolving that entire structure and replacing it with something radically different: a living, real-time, self-correcting tax system that operates quietly in the background of your financial life. Instead of you working for the tax system, the tax system is being rebuilt to work for you. This final book in the AI Personal Tax Optimization series explores how that transformation is unfolding, how it will impact every individual and household, and how those who understand it early will enjoy a future of unprecedented financial clarity, efficiency, and peace of mind.

In the old world, taxes were something you dealt with once a year, usually in a rush, often under pressure, and frequently with uncertainty about whether you had done everything correctly. The future powered by artificial intelligence looks nothing like that. AI systems are moving taxes from an annual event into a continuous, automated process that updates itself as you earn, spend, invest, and save. Every paycheck, every freelance payment, every crypto transaction, every real-estate deal, and every bank transfer can be interpreted, categorized, and evaluated instantly by algorithms that know the tax code better than any human ever could. Instead of discovering mistakes months later, the system corrects them in real time. Instead of guessing what you owe, you see it continuously. Instead of scrambling for deductions, the AI finds them automatically. Taxes no longer become a threat or a mystery; they become a predictable, optimized part of your financial ecosystem.

At the center of this future is the rise of fully automated tax filing. AI is already capable of assembling complete tax returns using data feeds from employers, banks, payment platforms, brokerages, crypto exchanges, and digital wallets. As this technology matures, filing a return will become less like filling out a form and more like confirming a dashboard. The system will already know your income, your expenses, your dependents, your credits, your investments, and your deductions. It will run millions of simulations to determine the optimal way to file and will present you with a finished return that has been mathematically optimized for compliance and savings. With a single click, that return will be transmitted securely to tax authorities. No stacks of receipts, no manual entries, no stress, no surprises.

The Internal Revenue Service itself is evolving into a digital, AI-driven institution. The future IRS will not operate primarily through letters, audits, and penalties, but through continuous data synchronization and algorithmic verification. Instead of reacting after the fact, AI-powered tax agencies will compare what you report with what financial institutions, employers, and platforms already know in real time. Discrepancies will be flagged immediately, often resolved automatically, and corrected before they ever become a problem. For honest taxpayers, this means fewer audits, fewer disputes, and far less fear. The IRS of the future is not an adversary but a data-driven partner that wants accurate information flowing seamlessly through the system.

This shift also means that tax planning will no longer be something you do at the end of the year or during a frantic meeting with an accountant. AI-powered tax forecasting tools will simulate the tax impact of every financial decision before you make it. Want to sell a property? The system will show you the tax outcome under multiple strategies. Thinking about exercising stock options? The AI will calculate the best timing. Considering a Roth conversion, a retirement contribution, or a charitable donation? The algorithms will instantly show you how to maximize your benefit. In this future, every decision is tax-aware, and every move is guided by predictive intelligence that keeps you in the optimal financial lane.

One of the most powerful implications of this future is the disappearance of most human error. Historically, the tax system has been filled with mistakes because it was designed for humans to process. AI changes that. Algorithms do not forget forms, miscalculate deductions, or misinterpret rules when they are properly trained. They operate with consistency and precision at a scale no person or firm could ever match. This dramatically reduces the risk of audits, penalties, and disputes, and it makes compliance easier than it has ever been. For individuals, this means that the anxiety that once accompanied tax season fades away, replaced by a sense of confidence that the system is working quietly and correctly on your behalf.

The future of AI-powered personal taxes is also deeply connected to financial inclusion. Millions of people today overpay taxes simply because they do not understand the rules or cannot afford professional help. AI makes high-level tax optimization accessible to everyone. A gig worker, a freelancer, a retiree, or a young family will have access to the same powerful planning tools once reserved for wealthy individuals and corporations. The technology does not discriminate; it simply computes. This creates a more fair and efficient system where people keep more of what they earn because the system finally works with them instead of against them.

As digital currencies, tokenized assets, and decentralized finance continue to grow, AI will become the only practical way to manage the tax complexity they create. Crypto transactions, NFT trades, staking rewards, and digital asset transfers generate enormous volumes of taxable data. No human could track this manually, but AI thrives in exactly this kind of environment. The future tax system will automatically classify digital transactions, calculate gains and losses, and integrate them seamlessly into your broader financial picture. What once seemed chaotic becomes structured, transparent, and manageable through intelligent automation.

Perhaps the most profound change of all is psychological. In a world of AI-powered taxes, people no longer fear the system. They do not dread the envelope from the government or the email from their accountant. They see their tax position at all times. They understand what they owe and why. They trust the numbers because they are continuously validated by machines that never get tired or distracted. This shift creates a new relationship between citizens and their financial obligations, one based on clarity, predictability, and control rather than confusion and stress. This book exists to help you understand that future before it fully arrives. The people who thrive in the next financial era will not be those who cling to old methods but those who learn how to work with intelligent systems that optimize every dollar they earn. By understanding how AI-driven tax platforms, digital IRS systems, real-time reporting, and automated compliance work, you position yourself ahead of the curve. You gain the ability to plan, invest, and build wealth with confidence, knowing that your tax foundation is solid, optimized, and always up to date.

AI Personal Tax Optimization is not science fiction. It is the logical outcome of data, automation, and intelligence converging into a single financial operating system for humanity. As you move through this final book in the series, you will see how all the tools, strategies, and concepts introduced in the previous volumes come together into one integrated vision of zero-stress, fully optimized personal taxation. The era of paperwork, panic, and penalties is ending. A new era of intelligent, invisible, and effortless taxation is beginning, and those who understand it now will enjoy a lifetime of greater financial freedom because of it.

Chapter 1

The Digital Tax Revolution

The digital tax revolution is not a single invention or a single software platform but a sweeping transformation that changes how money itself is understood, tracked, and taxed. For most of modern history, governments have tried to collect taxes using systems designed for paper, human labor, and delayed reporting. Artificial intelligence dissolves all of that. It introduces a new reality in which every financial event can be instantly recorded, interpreted, and optimized the moment it occurs. Income is no longer just a number on a paycheck or a line on a return; it becomes a real-time data stream. Expenses are no longer piles of receipts; they become automatically categorized signals. Investments are no longer seasonal summaries; they are continuously analyzed performance engines. The tax system of the future is built on this living financial data, and AI is the brain that makes sense of it.

In this new model, taxes stop being something you calculate after the year ends and instead become something that flows alongside your life. Every dollar you earn, spend, invest, or move triggers a micro-calculation inside intelligent software that understands the tax code better than any accountant ever could. These systems know how your income is classified, which deductions apply, how your assets are taxed, and what your future obligations will look like if nothing changes. They are not waiting for April; they are running nonstop. This continuous awareness allows people to see their true financial position at all times, removing the fear of unexpected tax bills and replacing it with clarity and control.

The power of this revolution comes from the way AI connects to the modern digital economy. Payroll platforms, payment processors, banks, investment accounts, crypto wallets, online marketplaces, and gig platforms all produce enormous amounts of structured financial data. Historically, most of this data sat in isolated silos and had to be manually pulled together once a year. AI breaks those walls down. It connects to everything, reads everything, and reconciles everything in real time. The result is a single, unified financial picture that is always up to date, always accurate, and always ready to be used for tax optimization.

One of the biggest changes this creates is the end of guesswork. In the old system, people often made financial decisions without knowing the tax impact until months later. You might sell an asset, take a side job, or make a big purchase without realizing how it would affect your tax bill. AI changes that by simulating outcomes instantly. Before you act, you can see what will happen. The system can show you how selling stock today versus next month affects your taxes, or how increasing your freelance income will change your withholding. Every choice becomes informed, deliberate, and strategically optimized.

This also transforms compliance. In the traditional system, compliance is reactive. You file your return, then wait to see if the government finds a problem. In an AI-driven system, compliance is proactive. The algorithms continuously check your data against the rules and correct issues as they appear. If income is misclassified, it is flagged and fixed. If a deduction is missing, it is added. If something looks inconsistent, it is resolved before it ever becomes a liability. This dramatically reduces audits, penalties, and disputes, making the entire system calmer and more cooperative.

The digital tax revolution also levels the playing field. For decades, wealthy individuals and corporations have had access to sophisticated tax planning tools, while ordinary people relied on basic software or human preparers. AI changes that imbalance. Once a system is built, it can be used by anyone. A freelancer, a rideshare driver, a retiree, or a small business owner can all benefit from the same advanced optimization strategies that used to require expensive professionals. This democratization of tax intelligence allows more people to keep more of what they earn simply because the system is finally smart enough to help them.

Security and transparency improve as well. AI-powered systems use encrypted data, audit trails, and continuous verification to ensure that every number is traceable and every calculation is justified. Instead of mysterious tax bills or unexplained adjustments, people can see exactly how their taxes were calculated and why. This builds trust in the system and reduces the anxiety that comes from not understanding how decisions were made. The tax system becomes not just more efficient, but more fair and understandable.

As governments modernize, they are also adopting AI to manage their own operations. The tax agencies of the future will not rely on random audits and human review alone. They will use intelligent systems to compare reported data with third-party sources, detect anomalies, and resolve discrepancies instantly. Honest taxpayers will experience fewer interruptions, while fraud and abuse will be identified more quickly and accurately. This creates a system that rewards compliance rather than punishing it.

The digital tax revolution is ultimately about shifting from a reactive, manual, fear-driven model to a proactive, automated, confidence-driven one. When AI handles the complexity, people are free to focus on their lives, their work, and their goals. Taxes become just another optimized part of the financial ecosystem, quietly working in the background. This is the foundation upon which the future of AI-powered personal taxes is being built, and it marks the beginning of a world where financial intelligence is always on your side.

"The Year Taxes Disappeared"

When Elena first noticed that she had not thought about taxes in months, it felt strange, almost unsettling. For most of her adult life, taxes had been a constant source of stress, looming in the background like an unpaid bill that never really went away. Every January, she would start collecting documents. Every March, she would panic. Every April, she would hope nothing was wrong. But now it was October, and she realized that the fear simply was not there anymore.

Elena was a freelance graphic designer, and her income used to be a mess of invoices, PayPal deposits, and client payments from half a dozen platforms. In the old days, she had tried to keep spreadsheets, but they were always incomplete. Then she started using an AI financial system that quietly connected to everything she used. It read every payment, categorized every expense, and tracked every deduction without her lifting a finger. What once felt chaotic became calm.

One afternoon, Elena decided to check her tax dashboard. It showed her estimated tax liability for the year, updated to the minute. She could see exactly how much she had already paid, how much she would likely owe, and what would happen if she took on more work before the end of the year. Out of curiosity, she adjusted a slider that represented future income. Instantly, the system showed her the tax impact. She realized she could accept a new client and still stay within her optimal bracket.

Later that week, Elena considered buying a new laptop for her business. In the past, she would have wondered if it was deductible and how it might affect her taxes. Now, she simply entered the price into her AI system. It calculated the deduction, adjusted her forecast, and told her exactly how much the purchase would reduce her tax bill. The decision became simple. She bought the laptop with confidence.

Months passed, and April arrived quietly. There were no frantic emails, no missing forms, no late nights sorting receipts. Her AI system notified her that her return was ready. Every number had already been verified against bank records, client reports, and platform data. The system had optimized her filing status, applied every credit, and chosen the best possible strategy for her situation. All Elena had to do was review and approve.

She clicked a button, and her return was filed. A confirmation appeared, along with her final tax outcome. It was lower than she had expected, not because she had done anything unusual, but because nothing had been missed. For the first time in her life, she felt that the tax system had worked for her instead of against her.

That night, Elena went out to dinner with friends. One of them complained about how stressful tax season had always been. Elena smiled and realized she no longer shared that feeling. Taxes had not disappeared, but the anxiety had. In its place was a quiet, invisible intelligence that handled the complexity while she lived her life. For her, and millions like her, the future had already arrived.

Chapter 2

The Rise of the Fully Automated Tax System

The rise of the fully automated tax system represents one of the most profound shifts in financial history, because it changes not only how taxes are calculated but how governments, businesses, and individuals interact with money itself. In the traditional world, tax systems were built around human effort, manual reporting, and delayed verification. People earned income all year long, but the system only reconciled it once, long after mistakes had already happened. Artificial intelligence replaces this fragile structure with a continuous, self-updating framework in which financial activity is captured, interpreted, and validated as it occurs. This shift transforms taxation from a stressful annual event into an invisible, always-on process that runs quietly in the background of everyday life.

At the heart of this system is real-time data integration. Every modern financial platform generates digital records: employers report payroll, banks track deposits, investment firms log trades, payment apps record transfers, and marketplaces track sales. In the past, these streams of data existed in isolation, forcing taxpayers to piece them together manually. AI unifies them into a single living ledger that reflects your true financial position at any moment. Income, expenses, investments, deductions, and credits are no longer separate fragments but parts of one coherent financial story that the system understands completely.

Once this data is unified, AI applies the tax code to it continuously. Instead of waiting for year-end calculations, algorithms interpret every transaction as it happens. If you earn freelance income, the system instantly classifies it. If you buy a deductible item, it is immediately recorded. If you sell an investment, the gain or loss is calculated on the spot. This constant interpretation means there are no surprises. You always know where you stand, and the system can adjust withholding, estimated payments, or savings recommendations in real time to keep you on track.

Automation also revolutionizes how returns are created. In the future, tax returns are not assembled by people or even by traditional software. They are generated automatically by systems that already possess all the necessary information. Your return becomes a summary of what the system already knows about your financial life. It is not something you build from scratch, but something you confirm. This reduces errors, eliminates missing information, and makes filing nearly effortless. The government side of this system evolves as well.

Tax agencies no longer need to guess or audit randomly. They receive synchronized, verified data from the same sources used by taxpayers. When your return is submitted, it is instantly compared against independent records. Discrepancies are resolved automatically or flagged for review. This makes enforcement more accurate and less intrusive, allowing honest taxpayers to move through the system without fear while ensuring that abuse is detected quickly.

Security is strengthened through this automation. AI systems use encryption, identity verification, and behavioral analysis to ensure that financial data is protected and that fraud is detected early. Suspicious activity, such as identity theft or false reporting, can be identified by patterns that humans would never notice. This creates a tax environment that is not only more efficient but safer for everyone involved.

The fully automated tax system also makes global and digital income manageable. As people earn money from international clients, online platforms, and digital assets, the complexity of taxation increases. AI thrives in this complexity. It can apply the correct rules to each type of income, track cross-border transactions, and ensure that everything is reported correctly. What once required specialized expertise becomes routine.

Perhaps most importantly, automation restores trust. When people can see that their taxes are calculated fairly, accurately, and transparently, they no longer feel like the system is working against them. They gain confidence that they are paying what they owe and not a dollar more. This trust encourages compliance and creates a healthier relationship between citizens and the financial systems that support society.

The rise of the fully automated tax system is not about replacing people; it is about freeing them. By removing manual labor, confusion, and fear from taxation, AI allows individuals to focus on building their lives, their businesses, and their futures. Taxes become a quiet, optimized service rather than a source of constant anxiety, and that change reshapes how people think about money itself.

"The Button That Filed Everything"

Marcus had always dreaded tax season. As a small business owner, he wore too many hats already, and taxes felt like one more burden he could never quite master. He used to spend weeks sorting receipts, logging expenses, and worrying that he had missed something. Every year ended with the same question in his mind: had he done it right.

Everything changed when his accounting software upgraded to a fully automated AI system. At first, Marcus did not trust it. The idea that a machine could handle something so important made him uneasy. But as months passed, he noticed something strange. His financial dashboard always made sense. Every sale, every expense, every payroll run was already categorized and accounted for. He could see his tax position at any moment.

One day in early spring, Marcus received a notification. His tax return was ready. He stared at the screen, waiting for the usual list of things he needed to provide, but there was nothing. The system already had everything. It had pulled data from his bank, his payment processor, his payroll service, and his expense cards. It had reconciled it all and built a complete, optimized return.

Marcus clicked through the summary. It showed his income, deductions, credits, and final tax liability. There were no mysteries, no missing numbers. Every figure had a clear source and explanation. He realized that for the first time in his life, he actually understood his taxes.

With a deep breath, he pressed the “File” button. In seconds, the return was sent to the government’s digital system. A confirmation appeared, followed by a projected refund.

Marcus leaned back in his chair, stunned by how simple it had been.

That evening, he went home feeling lighter than he had in years. Taxes had always felt like an enemy, but now they were just another automated process, quietly handled by intelligent software. The fear was gone, replaced by a calm confidence that everything was exactly as it should be.

Chapter 3

Real-Time Tax Intelligence

Real-time tax intelligence represents the final evolution of how people interact with money and government, because it transforms taxes from a delayed, backward-looking process into a living, forward-looking financial guide. In traditional systems, taxpayers only discovered their true tax situation after the year had already passed, which meant that many of their decisions were made blindly. Artificial intelligence changes this by turning every financial action into an immediate data point that is evaluated, classified, and optimized the moment it occurs. The result is a world in which you never wonder what your tax position is, because it is always visible, always updated, and always aligned with your financial goals.

At the core of this intelligence is continuous data flow. Every time you receive income, make a purchase, invest in an asset, or move money between accounts, AI systems capture that activity and instantly apply the tax code to it. They know what type of income it is, whether it is taxable, whether it qualifies for special treatment, and how it affects your overall tax picture. This happens quietly in the background, without forms or manual input, creating a tax awareness layer over your entire financial life.

This constant awareness allows AI to provide guidance that was never possible before. Instead of reacting after the fact, the system can advise you before you make a move. If you are about to sell stock, it can warn you about capital gains. If you are considering a freelance project, it can show you how it will change your estimated taxes. If you are thinking about a large purchase, it can calculate how much of it will be deductible. This turns the tax system into a strategic partner rather than a source of fear.

Real-time tax intelligence also reshapes how withholding and estimated payments work. In the old model, people either overpaid throughout the year or faced a large bill at the end because estimates were based on incomplete information. AI solves this by continuously adjusting your tax payments based on your actual activity. If your income increases, withholding rises. If it falls, withholding drops. The system keeps you balanced, preventing both painful surprises and unnecessary overpayments.

Another powerful benefit is audit prevention. Because the AI is constantly checking your data against known rules and third-party records, errors and inconsistencies are detected immediately. If something does not match, it is corrected before it ever becomes a problem. This dramatically reduces the chance of an audit, because the system itself enforces accuracy long before government agencies need to intervene.

Real-time intelligence also allows for deeper optimization. AI does not just follow the rules; it explores them. It can simulate thousands of possible strategies to find the one that produces the best result for you. It can recommend the best timing for income, the ideal structure for expenses, and the most efficient way to use credits and deductions. This kind of continuous optimization used to be available only to large corporations. Now it becomes accessible to everyone.

Transparency is another critical feature of this system. Every calculation, every classification, and every recommendation is traceable. You can see exactly how your taxes are being computed and why certain decisions are better than others. This builds trust and confidence, making it easier for people to understand and accept their financial obligations.

Real-time tax intelligence ultimately changes how people think about taxes. Instead of viewing them as a burden that appears once a year, people begin to see them as a dynamic part of their financial ecosystem, something that can be managed, optimized, and controlled. This shift in mindset is just as important as the technology itself, because it empowers individuals to take ownership of their financial future. As this technology becomes more widespread, the line between financial planning and tax planning disappears. AI integrates income, expenses, investments, and taxes into one coherent system that supports smarter decisions at every step. This is the true promise of real-time tax intelligence: a world in which every financial move is informed, optimized, and aligned with your long-term goals.

"The Day the Numbers Spoke"

Sofia had always been good with money, but taxes were the one thing she could never quite predict. As a consultant, her income changed from month to month, and every year she ended up either owing more than she expected or getting a refund that meant she had overpaid. It felt like a game she could never quite win.

That changed when her financial app introduced real-time tax intelligence. At first, it looked like a simple dashboard, but it quickly became something much more. It showed her not just her income and expenses, but her live tax position. Every time she got paid, the numbers shifted. Every time she spent money, the system adjusted.

One afternoon, Sofia was offered a new contract that would pay significantly more than her current work. Before she accepted, she checked her tax dashboard. The system showed her exactly how the extra income would affect her taxes and even suggested setting aside a certain amount to keep everything balanced. For the first time, she could see the future before it happened.

Later, she considered making a large charitable donation. In the past, she would have hoped it helped at tax time. Now, the system showed her instantly how much it would reduce her tax bill. The numbers spoke clearly, turning guesswork into certainty.

By the end of the year, Sofia noticed something remarkable. There were no surprises. Her estimated taxes matched her final numbers almost perfectly. When it was time to file, the return was already complete, built from the data the system had been tracking all along.

As she reviewed her results, Sofia felt a new kind of confidence. It was not just that her taxes were accurate; it was that she had been in control the whole time. The numbers had spoken, and for the first time, she had listened.

Chapter 4

Life Inside a Zero-Stress Tax System

A zero-stress tax system is not defined by the absence of taxes, but by the absence of uncertainty. Stress has never come from paying taxes themselves; it has always come from not knowing what you owe, why you owe it, or whether you have done something wrong. Artificial intelligence eliminates this uncertainty by transforming taxes into a continuously managed, transparent, and predictable process. In a zero-stress system, there are no hidden numbers, no last-minute discoveries, and no confusing notices that arrive months later. Everything is visible, calculated, and resolved as life unfolds.

The foundation of a zero-stress tax system is constant awareness. AI does not wait for you to prepare information or remember deadlines. It is always watching your financial activity, categorizing transactions, and applying the tax code in real time. This awareness removes the psychological burden that has historically followed taxpayers all year long. Instead of a vague sense that something important is being ignored, people gain a quiet confidence that the system is handling the complexity for them. This shift changes how people relate to money. When taxes are continuously tracked and optimized, income no longer feels risky or unpredictable. People stop hesitating to earn more because they are afraid of tax consequences they do not understand. AI shows them exactly what additional income means, how much will be owed, and how to plan for it. Growth becomes something to embrace rather than fear.

Zero-stress taxation also reshapes recordkeeping. The old model required people to save receipts, track mileage, log expenses, and remember details months later. AI removes this burden entirely. Transactions are recorded automatically at the source, enriched with contextual data, and stored securely. Every deduction is documented, every classification is justified, and every calculation is supported by data. When questions arise, the answers already exist.

Another critical element of this system is early resolution. In the past, mistakes often went unnoticed until a return was filed or an audit occurred. AI identifies issues immediately. If income is misreported by a third party, the system flags it. If an expense is categorized incorrectly, it corrects it. Problems are solved while they are small, preventing them from becoming stressful events later.

Communication with tax authorities also changes dramatically. Instead of letters written in technical language, people interact with clear digital explanations. AI systems translate tax concepts into plain language, explaining what happened and what needs to be done. This removes fear and confusion, replacing them with understanding and cooperation.

A zero-stress system is also adaptive. Life changes constantly. People change jobs, start businesses, invest, relocate, and retire. AI systems adjust instantly, recalculating tax strategies based on new circumstances. There is no lag time, no learning curve, and no need to re-educate the system. It evolves with you.

Perhaps the most important outcome of a zero-stress tax system is emotional relief. When people no longer fear tax season, they reclaim mental space and energy. They think more clearly about goals, savings, investments, and family plans. Taxes become a solved problem rather than a recurring crisis.

This chapter represents the culmination of everything discussed so far. Real-time intelligence, automation, and integration converge to create an environment where taxes simply work. The zero-stress tax system is not about avoiding responsibility; it is about removing friction so responsibility becomes effortless. This is the lived experience of the future, and it is closer than most people realize.

"April Without Fear"

For most of her life, April had been the month Nadia dreaded more than any other. Even as a child, she remembered her parents arguing over paperwork at the kitchen table, stacks of envelopes spread everywhere, tension hanging in the air. As an adult, nothing had changed. The fear had simply become hers.

Nadia worked in marketing, earned bonuses that fluctuated year to year, and invested on the side. She was organized, careful, and responsible, yet tax season always made her feel like she was one mistake away from disaster. She never knew if she had saved enough, deducted enough, or reported everything correctly. The stress lingered for months.

Then her financial platform quietly transitioned to a fully AI-managed tax system. At first, Nadia barely noticed. The interface looked cleaner. The summaries were clearer. But over time, something deeper changed. The fear started to fade.

By midsummer, she realized she could see her tax position whenever she wanted. It wasn't just a number. It was a story. It showed her income streams, explained how each was taxed, and projected outcomes months into the future. The system even alerted her gently when something required attention, always with a clear explanation and a suggested solution. In September, Nadia received an unexpected bonus. Normally, this would have triggered anxiety. This time, her phone buzzed with a notification. The system showed her exactly how the bonus affected her taxes and recommended an adjustment to her withholding. She followed the suggestion, and the anxiety never arrived.

As the year went on, Nadia stopped thinking about taxes altogether. There was no reason to. She focused on her work, her health, and her family. The system handled the rest.

Then April came.

It arrived quietly, without panic or urgency. One morning, Nadia received a message: "Your return is ready for review." She hesitated, expecting the familiar rush of stress, but it never came. She opened the dashboard.

Everything was there. Every paycheck. Every investment trade. Every deduction. Each number had an explanation written in language she could understand. The system showed her what she owed, why she owed it, and how it compared to projections from months earlier. Nothing was surprising.

She clicked through the details slowly, almost ceremonially. For the first time, filing taxes felt less like a test and more like a confirmation. When she approved the return, the system filed it instantly. A confirmation appeared, followed by a calm message: "Filed successfully. No action needed."

Nadia sat back in her chair, stunned by how ordinary it felt. No fear. No rush. No lingering doubt.

That evening, she went for a walk. The air felt lighter. She realized that April had lost its power over her. Taxes were no longer something that haunted her once a year. They were simply part of the background, managed, optimized, and understood.

For Nadia, the future wasn't about paying less or earning more. It was about living without fear. And for the first time, she knew that fear was gone for good.

Chapter 5

Trust, Transparency, and the New Relationship With Taxes

For generations, the relationship between individuals and the tax system has been shaped by mistrust. Taxpayers assumed the system was too complex to fully understand, while tax authorities assumed errors or noncompliance were inevitable. This mutual suspicion created an environment where fear, confusion, and defensiveness became normal. Artificial intelligence fundamentally rewires this relationship by introducing something that was largely missing before: continuous transparency. When every calculation can be seen, explained, verified, and traced back to its source, trust stops being an abstract idea and becomes a daily experience.

Transparency in an AI-powered tax system begins with visibility. Instead of seeing taxes as a black box that produces a number once a year, individuals can see every step of the process as it happens. Income is not just reported; it is explained. Expenses are not just deducted; they are justified. Credits are not just applied; they are contextualized. This visibility removes the feeling that something is being hidden or manipulated behind the scenes. People no longer feel like passive participants in a system they do not understand. They become informed observers of a process that makes logical sense.

Trust grows when explanations are clear. AI systems excel at translating complexity into plain language. When a tax rule applies, the system can explain why, how it was applied, and what alternatives might exist. This level of explanation has historically been unavailable to most taxpayers, who relied on professionals or vague software prompts. With AI, understanding is no longer reserved for experts. It becomes embedded into the system itself, empowering individuals to learn simply by observing how their own taxes are handled.

This transparency also changes how mistakes are perceived. In the traditional system, errors often felt catastrophic because they were discovered late and communicated harshly. In an AI-driven environment, mistakes are identified early and corrected quietly. The system flags an inconsistency, explains it, and resolves it before it escalates. This transforms errors from sources of fear into routine maintenance tasks, similar to correcting a typo in a document. The emotional weight disappears because the consequences are managed proactively.

Trust also extends to data integrity. People are understandably cautious about sharing financial information, but AI-powered systems rely on robust security, encryption, and verification protocols that exceed what manual systems could ever provide. Every data point has a source. Every change is logged. Every calculation can be audited instantly. This creates a level of accountability that builds confidence not just in the results, but in the system itself.

As trust increases, behavior changes. When people believe the system is fair and accurate, they are more willing to comply and engage. They stop looking for shortcuts or avoiding information. Instead, they collaborate with the system, using its insights to make better decisions. This cooperative dynamic benefits everyone. Individuals pay what they owe with confidence, and governments receive more accurate data with fewer enforcement costs.

Transparency also reshapes long-term planning. When people trust the numbers they see, they can plan years into the future without fear that hidden tax consequences will derail their goals. Retirement planning, investment strategies, career changes, and major purchases all become more approachable when taxes are no longer an unpredictable variable. AI provides not just answers, but reassurance.

This new relationship with taxes is not about blind faith in technology. It is about verifiable clarity. People do not trust the system because it is intelligent; they trust it because it is understandable. Every output is supported by logic, data, and explanation. This alignment between intelligence and transparency is what finally dissolves decades of mistrust.

As AI-powered tax systems become the norm, the cultural narrative around taxes will shift. Taxes will no longer be seen as something done to people, but something done with them. This partnership mindset marks a turning point in financial history, one where trust replaces fear and transparency replaces confusion. It is not just a technical upgrade. It is a relational transformation.

"Nothing to Hide"

Daniel had always believed that taxes were designed to trick people. Not necessarily out of malice, but out of complexity. He grew up hearing stories about audits, penalties, and fines that came out of nowhere. His parents paid their taxes faithfully, yet they were always anxious, always worried that something had been missed. That anxiety settled into Daniel early, shaping how he viewed money and authority.

As an adult, Daniel did everything "right." He worked a stable job, invested carefully, and used reputable tax software. Still, every year he felt the same unease when filing. He clicked through screens he barely understood, trusted calculations he couldn't explain, and submitted returns with a quiet hope that nothing would come back to haunt him. He never felt confident, only relieved when it was over.

When his employer introduced a new AI-driven financial platform that integrated taxes directly into payroll and personal finances, Daniel was skeptical. The promise sounded too good to be true: complete transparency, real-time explanations, and no surprises. He assumed it was just marketing language.

The first time he noticed something different was subtle. After receiving a paycheck, Daniel checked the dashboard and saw not just the net amount, but a breakdown of how taxes were calculated. Each line item had a short explanation written in plain language. He clicked one out of curiosity and found a clear description of why that amount was withheld and how it aligned with his projected annual income.

Over the next few weeks, Daniel started checking the dashboard more often. It wasn't because he was worried; it was because he was curious. The system didn't just show numbers. It told a story. It showed how his contributions to retirement accounts affected his taxes. It explained how his investment dividends were classified. It even flagged a small discrepancy between a bank report and his records, explained the issue, and resolved it automatically.

For the first time, Daniel felt like the system was talking to him, not at him.

One evening, he decided to explore the tax simulation feature. He adjusted hypothetical scenarios: a raise, a side project, a large purchase. Each time, the system recalculated his tax outlook and explained the changes. There was no judgment, no warnings, just clear information. The more he explored, the more his old fear began to dissolve.

Months later, Daniel received a notification: "Minor adjustment resolved." In the past, this kind of message would have triggered panic. This time, he opened it calmly. The system explained that a third-party report had slightly misclassified income, showed the correction, and confirmed that no action was needed. Daniel felt something unfamiliar—trust.

When tax season arrived, there was no buildup of dread. His return was already prepared, complete with a detailed walkthrough of every calculation. Daniel reviewed it slowly, not because he was afraid, but because he finally understood it. Each section made sense. Nothing felt hidden.

As he approved the filing, Daniel realized something profound. For the first time in his life, he felt like he had nothing to hide—not because he had done everything perfectly, but because the system itself was transparent. There were no traps, no secrets, no sudden surprises waiting in the shadows.

Later that night, Daniel thought about his parents and the stress they carried year after year. He wished they could see this future, where taxes were no longer an adversarial process but an open, understandable one. Where trust was built not on faith, but on clarity.

As he closed his laptop, Daniel smiled. The fear that had followed him for decades was gone. In its place was a quiet confidence rooted in transparency. For the first time, the system felt fair—not because it demanded trust, but because it earned it.

Chapter 6

AI as Your Personal Tax Co-Pilot

The next stage in the evolution of AI-powered personal taxes is not just automation or transparency, but guidance. Artificial intelligence is no longer limited to calculating what already happened; it is becoming an active participant in shaping what happens next. In this role, AI functions as a personal tax co-pilot, quietly sitting beside you as you earn, spend, invest, and plan, continuously offering insight without demanding attention. This shift fundamentally changes how people experience taxes, turning them from a reactive obligation into a proactive decision-support system woven into everyday life.

A tax co-pilot does not wait for you to ask questions. It anticipates them. By observing patterns in income, expenses, savings, and investments, AI learns how your financial life behaves over time. It understands seasonality, career changes, lifestyle shifts, and risk tolerance. Using this understanding, it can recognize when a decision you are about to make has tax consequences and surface that information at the exact moment it matters. This is not about alerts or warnings, but about timely clarity delivered when it can actually influence outcomes. One of the most powerful aspects of an AI tax co-pilot is contextual awareness. Traditional tax tools treat every year as a separate event. AI sees continuity. It understands where you came from, where you are now, and where you are likely headed. It can identify long-term opportunities that are invisible in a single-year snapshot, such as spreading income across years, timing asset sales, or adjusting retirement strategies gradually rather than reactively. This long-range perspective transforms tax planning into a continuous, intelligent process rather than a rushed annual exercise.

This guidance extends beyond saving money. A tax co-pilot also protects people from unintended consequences. Many financial mistakes are not reckless; they are uninformed. People accept bonuses, sell assets, or take side income without realizing how those actions ripple through their tax situation. AI intervenes gently, showing the implications before the decision is finalized. It does not tell you what to do; it shows you what will happen. This preserves autonomy while eliminating blind spots.

Another defining feature of the tax co-pilot is personalization. No two financial lives are identical, and AI systems are uniquely capable of adapting to individual circumstances. The guidance offered to a salaried employee will differ from that offered to a freelancer, investor, or retiree. Even within the same category, AI adjusts recommendations based on goals, habits, and preferences. This level of customization was once only available through high-touch advisory services. Now it becomes accessible to anyone with digital financial data.

The presence of a tax co-pilot also changes emotional behavior. When people feel guided rather than judged, they engage more deeply with their finances. Instead of avoiding tax topics out of fear, they explore them out of curiosity. The system becomes a source of reassurance rather than anxiety. This emotional shift leads to better decisions, not because people are forced to comply, but because they feel supported.

Importantly, the tax co-pilot does not replace human judgment or values. It provides information, scenarios, and projections, but the final choice always belongs to the individual. AI offers clarity, not commands. This balance preserves personal agency while dramatically improving decision quality. People remain in control, but they are no longer operating in the dark.

As AI co-pilots become more sophisticated, they will integrate taxes seamlessly with broader financial planning. Income decisions will align with investment strategies. Spending choices will reflect long-term goals. Retirement planning will incorporate tax efficiency automatically. The artificial boundaries between budgeting, investing, and taxation will dissolve, replaced by a single intelligent system that understands the whole picture. This chapter represents a turning point in the relationship between people and taxes. When AI steps into the role of co-pilot, taxes stop being something you manage alone. You are no longer navigating complexity without a map. Instead, you move forward with constant, quiet guidance that helps you make smarter decisions every step of the way. This is not just better tax software. It is a new way of living financially informed.

"The Quiet Voice in the Background"

Ethan never thought of himself as bad with money, but he always felt slightly behind it. Not struggling, not reckless, just perpetually unsure. He earned a good living in product design, invested modestly, and saved consistently, yet every major financial decision came with hesitation. He worried about timing, consequences, and hidden tax implications he didn't fully understand.

When his financial platform introduced an AI tax co-pilot, Ethan didn't expect much. He assumed it would be another layer of notifications he would eventually ignore. But from the beginning, it felt different. The system didn't interrupt him. It waited.

The first time it spoke up was subtle. Ethan was reviewing a contract for a freelance project on the side. As he scrolled through the payment terms, a small message appeared on his dashboard: "This income will shift your projected tax balance. Would you like to see options?" There was no alarm, no urgency. Just an invitation.

Curious, Ethan clicked. The screen showed three scenarios. One involved taking the full payment immediately. Another spread the income across two quarters. The third suggested adjusting withholding slightly to keep everything balanced. Each option showed clear outcomes, explained in simple language. For the first time, Ethan felt like he could choose rather than guess. He selected the option that fit his goals and moved on with confidence.

Over the next few months, the co-pilot appeared only when it mattered. When Ethan considered selling a small batch of stock, it showed him how waiting a few weeks would change the tax treatment. When he increased his retirement contribution, it explained how the decision reduced his current tax burden while strengthening his future. Each time, the guidance felt timely, never intrusive.

What surprised Ethan most was how the system learned. It noticed that he preferred stability over aggressive optimization. It adjusted its suggestions accordingly. It stopped presenting extreme scenarios and focused on balanced ones. The guidance felt increasingly personal, almost intuitive. As the year progressed, Ethan stopped feeling tense about money. Not because he thought about it more, but because he thought about it less. The co-pilot was always there, watching quietly, ready to speak if needed. He didn't feel managed. He felt accompanied.

One evening, Ethan sat down to review his financial summary. The dashboard showed not just numbers, but a narrative of the year. Decisions he had made, opportunities he had taken, risks he had avoided. The tax outcome aligned almost perfectly with projections from months earlier. There were no surprises, no regrets.

When tax season arrived, it felt anticlimactic. The return was already complete, built from a year of guided decisions. Ethan reviewed it slowly, recognizing moments when the co-pilot had nudged him just enough to change an outcome. Each nudge now made sense.

After filing, Ethan leaned back and reflected on how different the year had felt. There had been no panic, no second-guessing, no late-night searches trying to understand tax rules. He realized that the biggest change wasn't financial. It was psychological.

For the first time, Ethan felt like he wasn't alone in managing complexity. There was a quiet intelligence in the background, not controlling his life, not judging his choices, just helping him see clearly. That quiet voice never demanded attention, but it was always there when he needed it.

As he closed his laptop, Ethan smiled. He hadn't outsourced responsibility. He had gained perspective. And in that partnership between human intention and artificial intelligence, he finally felt in control of his financial future.

Chapter 7

Preparing for a World of Invisible Taxes

The most transformative feature of the future tax system is not speed, automation, or even intelligence, but invisibility. Invisible taxes do not mean hidden taxes or unaccountable systems. They mean taxes that no longer demand attention because they are seamlessly integrated into everyday financial life. Just as people no longer think about how email routes messages across the globe or how GPS calculates directions, the future taxpayer will no longer think about calculations, forms, deadlines, or filings. Artificial intelligence absorbs those responsibilities, allowing taxation to operate as a background utility rather than a foreground burden.

Preparing for a world of invisible taxes begins with understanding that the tax system is no longer an isolated annual ritual. It is becoming a continuous infrastructure layer that sits beneath income, spending, investing, and saving. Every financial action already produces digital data. AI simply connects that data to rules, logic, and outcomes in real time. This integration means that taxes no longer interrupt life; they flow with it. The anxiety that once accompanied financial growth fades because consequences are known immediately, not discovered months later.

This invisibility changes behavior in subtle but profound ways. When people no longer fear tax season, they become more willing to pursue opportunities. They take on new projects, invest more confidently, and make career moves without worrying about hidden penalties or surprises. Economic activity becomes more fluid because the system provides constant feedback instead of delayed punishment. Growth feels safer when uncertainty is removed.

Invisible taxation also requires a shift in mindset. People must learn to trust systems that operate quietly and continuously. This does not mean blind trust, but informed trust built on transparency and verification. AI-powered systems provide dashboards, explanations, and audit trails for those who want them, but they do not force engagement. The system is always available, but never intrusive. This balance between visibility and invisibility is what makes the new model sustainable.

Another important aspect of preparing for invisible taxes is understanding that compliance becomes automatic rather than intentional. In the past, compliance required effort: gathering documents, meeting deadlines, and interpreting rules. In the future, compliance happens by default because the system already has accurate data and applies the rules continuously. People do not become compliant by trying harder; they become compliant by living normally within a system that is designed to work correctly.

Governments also prepare for this shift by redesigning their role. Tax authorities move from enforcement-based models to verification-based models. Instead of catching mistakes after the fact, they validate data in real time. This reduces the need for audits, penalties, and adversarial interactions. The relationship becomes more collaborative, focused on accuracy rather than punishment.

Invisible taxes also reshape education. Instead of learning tax rules through stressful experiences or complex instructions, people learn organically by observing how their financial system behaves. When someone earns income, the system shows the impact. When they make a decision, the system explains the outcome. Learning becomes passive, contextual, and continuous rather than forced and abstract.

As invisible taxes become the norm, the concept of tax season itself begins to disappear. There is no dramatic moment of reckoning because everything has already been reconciled. Filing becomes a formality, often automated entirely. Refunds and payments are small adjustments rather than large surprises. The emotional peak that once defined tax season flattens into a steady, predictable experience.

Preparing for this world is not about mastering new tools; it is about letting go of old habits. People must release the belief that taxes are inherently stressful, confusing, or adversarial. Those beliefs were artifacts of outdated systems. AI-powered invisibility replaces them with predictability, clarity, and calm. The system does not demand attention because it no longer needs correction.

This chapter represents a threshold moment. Invisible taxes are not a distant future; they are emerging now. Those who understand and accept this shift will experience financial life differently. They will spend less time worrying and more time building. They will see taxes not as a burden to manage, but as a solved problem quietly handled in the background. This is the final step in the evolution of personal taxation, and it redefines what financial freedom truly feels like.

"The Last Tax Season"

No one noticed when it happened.

There was no announcement, no headline, no official declaration that tax season was over forever. It simply... faded. Like a tradition that quietly lost its meaning, April came and went without the usual tension. At first, people thought it was coincidence. Then they realized it was something else entirely.

For Laura, the realization came on an ordinary Tuesday

morning.

She was drinking coffee, scrolling through emails, when a notification appeared from her financial app. It was calm, understated, almost boring.

"Annual tax reconciliation complete. No action required."

Laura frowned slightly. She opened the message, expecting instructions, attachments, or warnings. There were none. Just a summary. Income verified. Expenses categorized. Investments reconciled. Compliance confirmed.

She stared at the screen longer than necessary.

Tax season was over.

At least, for her.

Laura worked as a product manager at a mid-sized tech company. Her finances weren't simple. She had salary income, bonuses, investments, a rental property she shared with her sister, and a side consulting contract she took on occasionally. For years, this complexity had made tax season a source of dread. She used to mark April on her calendar like a storm warning.

But something had changed gradually, almost invisibly.

Months earlier, her company had transitioned payroll to an AI-integrated financial system. Her bank had followed. Her investment platform upgraded next. Each step felt minor at the time. A cleaner dashboard. Better explanations. Fewer forms.

Now, sitting at her kitchen table, Laura realized she hadn't thought about taxes in months.

She opened her financial dashboard out of curiosity. Everything was there, neatly organized, quietly complete. Her tax position wasn't a mystery or a looming obligation. It was just another data point, stable and predictable. She scrolled through the timeline of the year and saw how each decision had already been accounted for. When she received a bonus, the system adjusted automatically. When she repaired the rental property, deductions were applied in real time. When she sold a small investment, the impact had been calculated the same day.

There had been no drama. No scramble. No fear.

Later that week, Laura met her father for lunch. He had retired a few years earlier and still carried the habits of a different era. As they ate, he mentioned that he needed to "get started on taxes soon."

Laura paused.

“Oh,” she said carefully, “I already filed.”

Her father raised an eyebrow. “Already? It’s barely April.”

She shrugged. “I didn’t really file. It was... done.”

He laughed, assuming she was exaggerating, but Laura didn’t laugh back. She tried to explain. The system tracked everything. Adjusted automatically. Filed digitally. No paperwork. No stress.

Her father listened quietly, then shook his head. “I don’t trust something that easy.”

Laura understood. She used to feel the same way.

That night, she thought about all the Aprils of her past. The late nights, the anxiety, the uncertainty. The fear of letters arriving unexpectedly. The sense that she was always behind, always missing something.

She realized that fear had shaped her financial behavior more than she ever admitted. It had made her cautious, hesitant, sometimes even avoidant. And now, without that fear, something else had emerged: confidence.

The next month, Laura accepted a new consulting opportunity without hesitation. The system showed her exactly how it would affect her taxes. No guessing. No dread. Just information. By summer, she barely noticed tax-related notifications anymore. They were there if she wanted them, but she didn't need to engage. Everything worked.

In the fall, a coworker mentioned how stressful tax season was approaching. Laura blinked, momentarily confused. Then she realized what he meant.

Tax season.

The phrase felt outdated, like something from another time.

That winter, as the year closed, Laura received another notification. "Year-end reconciliation complete. Estimated outcome confirmed."

She smiled, closed the app, and went on with her evening.

There was no dramatic ending to tax season. No celebration. No announcement.

It simply stopped being a problem.

And in that quiet disappearance, Laura understood the true promise of the future. Not freedom from responsibility, but freedom from fear. Not avoidance, but effortless compliance. Not chaos, but calm.

The last tax season hadn't ended with fireworks.

It ended with silence.

And that silence changed everything.

Chapter 8

Designing a Life Around Effortless Compliance

Effortless compliance is the quiet endpoint of the AI tax evolution, where living responsibly and being compliant are no longer separate actions but the same thing. For most of modern history, compliance required conscious effort. People had to remember rules, track documentation, meet deadlines, and interpret regulations that were never designed for everyday understanding. Artificial intelligence dissolves that separation by embedding compliance directly into daily financial behavior. In this new paradigm, people do not "do taxes" any more than they "do electricity." The system works continuously, invisibly, and reliably as part of life itself.

Designing a life around effortless compliance begins with recognizing that most noncompliance has never been intentional. Errors happened because systems were fragmented, information was delayed, and rules were too complex to apply manually. AI solves this by synchronizing data at the source. Income is reported when earned. Expenses are documented when incurred. Investments are classified when traded. Compliance no longer depends on memory or discipline; it depends on system design. When the system is intelligent, compliance becomes automatic.

This shift profoundly alters personal responsibility. Responsibility no longer means constant vigilance; it means choosing systems that work correctly. When individuals connect their financial lives to AI-driven platforms, they are not surrendering control but exercising it at a higher level. They are deciding to live within an infrastructure that enforces accuracy continuously rather than retroactively. This is a more mature form of responsibility, one that prioritizes outcomes over effort.

Effortless compliance also changes how people plan their lives. When tax obligations are predictable and continuously managed, long-term decisions become clearer. Career changes, entrepreneurship, investments, relocations, and retirement planning no longer carry hidden compliance risks. AI systems model these transitions in advance, showing how rules apply across time and circumstances. The fear of accidentally violating a regulation fades because the system adapts instantly as life changes.

Another critical element of effortless compliance is normalization. When everyone operates within intelligent systems, compliance stops feeling like a moral test and starts feeling like a default state. There is no stigma, no anxiety, and no adversarial tone. People are compliant because the system makes it easy to be compliant, not because they are afraid of punishment. This normalization leads to higher overall accuracy and fairness across society.

Effortless compliance also reshapes the role of education. Instead of learning tax rules abstractly, people learn by observing outcomes in their own lives. When an action has a tax consequence, the system explains it. When a rule applies, it shows why. This experiential learning builds understanding organically over time. People become financially literate not through stress, but through exposure to clear, contextual information.

From the perspective of government, effortless compliance reduces enforcement costs dramatically. When systems verify data continuously, there is less need for audits, penalties, and investigations. Resources shift from policing to maintaining system integrity and updating rules. This creates a healthier ecosystem where compliance is achieved through design rather than force.

Emotionally, designing life around effortless compliance creates calm. The constant background anxiety that once accompanied financial responsibility disappears. People stop bracing for mistakes and start trusting the system that supports them. This emotional relief has ripple effects, improving decision-making, mental health, and overall well-being.

Effortless compliance is not about removing accountability; it is about aligning accountability with reality. In a digital world where financial data already exists, requiring people to manually reconstruct it is inefficient and unnecessary. AI restores alignment between how life actually happens and how it is regulated. This alignment is the true innovation.

As this chapter concludes, it becomes clear that effortless compliance is not a technical achievement alone. It is a lifestyle shift. Those who embrace it will experience a different relationship with responsibility, one that is quieter, steadier, and far less stressful. Compliance will no longer be something you worry about. It will simply be the way your life operates.

"Nothing Left to Prove"

Maya used to believe that responsibility had to feel heavy.

She had grown up watching adults around her equate responsibility with stress. Bills were paid with sighs. Paperwork was handled late at night. Taxes, in particular, were treated like a trial—something you endured, something you survived. Responsibility meant vigilance, and vigilance meant exhaustion. By the time Maya was thirty-five, she was doing well by every external measure. She worked in healthcare operations, earned a strong income, invested consistently, and supported her younger brother through college. Yet beneath that success was a constant hum of anxiety. She worried not about money itself, but about compliance—whether she was doing things correctly, whether she had overlooked something, whether a mistake would surface years later and unravel her sense of control.

The anxiety didn't spike dramatically. It lingered. Quiet. Persistent.

When her employer transitioned to an AI-driven financial ecosystem, Maya barely noticed at first. Payroll changed providers. Benefits dashboards updated. Her bank integrated new tools. None of it felt revolutionary. It just felt... smoother.

Over time, small things began to shift.

When Maya received a performance bonus, the system adjusted her withholding automatically. No forms. No decisions. Just a brief explanation she could read if she wanted to. When she paid tuition for her brother, the system categorized it, explained the limits, and documented everything instantly. When she sold a small investment to cover unexpected expenses, the tax implications appeared clearly, already accounted for.

There were no warnings. No alarms.

Just clarity.

Months passed, and Maya realized something unsettling: she hadn't worried about compliance in a long time. The fear that once lived in the background had gone quiet. She kept waiting for it to return, convinced that calm must be temporary.

Then April approached.

Maya noticed coworkers beginning to talk about tax season. Complaints surfaced in meetings. Jokes about paperwork and deadlines made the rounds. She listened politely, but the conversations felt strangely distant, like people discussing a storm she wasn't expecting.

One evening, she opened her financial dashboard. A notification sat calmly at the top.

"Annual compliance verified. No action required."

She read it twice.

No action required.

Her return wasn't "prepared." It wasn't "almost ready." It was complete. Filed digitally. Verified across all connected sources. Every number reconciled. Every rule applied. Nothing outstanding.

Maya felt a strange mix of relief and disbelief. She searched for something to fix, something to double-check. There was nothing.

That night, she called her mother.

"Have you started your taxes yet?" Maya asked.

Her mother laughed tiredly. "Not yet. I'm dreading it."

Maya hesitated before responding. "Mine are already done."

There was a pause on the line. "Already?"

"I didn't really do anything," Maya said slowly. "They were just... done."

Her mother didn't know what to say.

After the call, Maya sat quietly, reflecting. For years, she had believed that being responsible meant proving it constantly. Checking. Rechecking. Worrying. Carrying the weight of compliance as a badge of adulthood.

Now she realized something profound.

Responsibility didn't have to hurt.

The system wasn't making her less accountable. It was making accountability effortless. Her financial life was accurate not because she was vigilant, but because the infrastructure around her was intelligent. She hadn't abdicated responsibility. She had redesigned it.

In the weeks that followed, Maya noticed changes in herself. She made decisions faster, without fear. She accepted a leadership role at work without worrying about tax complexity. She began planning for the future with excitement instead of hesitation.

One afternoon, as she closed her laptop after reviewing her financial summary, Maya felt something she hadn't felt in years.

Peace.

There was nothing left to prove. No looming deadline. No hidden risk waiting to surface.

Compliance wasn't something she chased anymore.

It was simply the way her life worked.

And for the first time, responsibility felt light enough to carry.

Chapter 9

Financial Freedom in an AI-Managed World

Financial freedom has traditionally been defined as a destination: a certain net worth, a certain income level, or a point at which work becomes optional. In an AI-managed world, financial freedom begins to take on a deeper and more practical meaning. It is no longer only about how much money you have, but about how little friction, uncertainty, and mental overhead your financial life contains. Artificial intelligence reshapes freedom by removing the invisible burdens that once consumed time, attention, and emotional energy—especially around taxes and compliance.

In the past, even financially successful people often lived with constant financial tension. High income brought complexity. Investments brought reporting obligations. Growth brought risk. Taxes loomed as an unpredictable force capable of undoing progress through mistakes or misunderstandings. AI dissolves this tension by creating continuity. When finances are tracked, interpreted, and optimized continuously, freedom emerges not from escape, but from alignment. Income, taxes, savings, and goals move together in harmony. An AI-managed financial system gives people something they rarely had before: certainty. Certainty about what they owe, why they owe it, and what will happen next. This certainty changes behavior. People no longer delay decisions out of fear. They no longer under-earn to avoid complexity. They no longer overpay just to stay safe. Instead, they act with confidence, knowing that the system will absorb complexity and surface clarity when needed.

This confidence is the foundation of modern financial freedom. When people trust that their financial system is accurate and adaptive, they stop micromanaging it. They stop obsessing over details and start focusing on direction. AI handles execution; humans focus on intention. This division of labor is what allows financial life to feel expansive rather than restrictive.

AI also democratizes freedom. Historically, true financial optimization was reserved for those who could afford advisors, planners, and specialists. Everyone else navigated complexity alone. AI collapses that divide. Once intelligent systems are built, they scale effortlessly. The same optimization logic that benefits a high-net-worth investor can also benefit a freelancer, a family, or a retiree. Financial freedom becomes less about privilege and more about access to intelligence.

Another profound shift occurs in how people relate to time. Traditional financial management required periodic attention bursts—tax season, quarterly estimates, year-end planning. These interruptions fragmented life. AI smooths time by distributing management evenly across the year. There are no spikes of stress or urgency because nothing accumulates unnoticed. This temporal smoothness is a quiet but powerful form of freedom.

AI-managed systems also support values-based living. When financial outcomes are predictable and optimized, people can align money with purpose more easily. They can donate strategically, invest intentionally, and design lifestyles that reflect their priorities rather than reacting to financial pressure. Freedom becomes not just the absence of constraint, but the presence of choice.

Importantly, AI does not remove responsibility from individuals. It reframes it. Responsibility shifts from manual execution to strategic oversight. People remain accountable for goals, ethics, and decisions, but they are no longer burdened with mechanical tasks that obscure the bigger picture. This reframing elevates human agency instead of diminishing it.

In an AI-managed world, financial freedom is no longer a finish line you cross someday. It is a condition you experience daily. It feels like calm awareness instead of constant vigilance. It feels like momentum instead of friction. It feels like confidence without arrogance and security without stagnation.

This chapter makes one truth clear: when taxes, compliance, and optimization are handled continuously by intelligent systems, money stops being a source of fear and starts being a tool. And when money becomes a tool rather than a threat, freedom stops being abstract. It becomes real, lived, and sustainable.

"The Weight She Didn't Know She Was Carrying"

Claire had always described herself as "doing fine."

She paid her bills on time. She saved regularly. She invested conservatively. From the outside, her life looked stable and well-managed. Friends came to her for advice because she seemed calm about money, organized, responsible.

What Claire didn't realize was how much effort that calm required.

Every decision carried weight. A promotion meant higher taxes. A bonus meant recalculating savings. A new investment meant paperwork, reporting, and the quiet fear that she might misunderstand something important. None of this overwhelmed her outright, but it accumulated slowly, like tension in muscles you don't realize are clenched.

Claire worked in corporate strategy and earned a strong income. Her financial life had grown more complex over the years, not because she chased risk, but because she progressed. And with each step forward, she carried more invisible responsibility.

She told herself this was normal. Adulthood, she believed, was supposed to feel heavy.

When her financial institution rolled out a fully AI-managed financial system, Claire paid polite attention and moved on. She had seen upgrades before. New dashboards. New terminology. Nothing ever really changed.

This time, though, change arrived quietly.

At first, it felt like nothing. Her accounts synced automatically. Transactions were categorized instantly. She noticed explanations appearing beside numbers, but she rarely clicked them. Life continued as usual.

Then one day, Claire declined an opportunity she would normally have taken. A short-term consulting role offered extra income, but she hesitated. The tax implications felt unclear, and she didn't want to complicate things.

Later that evening, she opened her financial dashboard, not with intention, but out of habit. A small prompt appeared.

"Would you like to see the impact of additional income this quarter?"

Claire clicked.

The system showed her exactly what would happen. No vague estimates. No warnings. Just clear outcomes. It showed how much she would earn, how much would be withheld, and how the additional income would affect her year overall. It even suggested an optimal allocation that kept everything balanced.

Claire felt something loosen in her chest.

She accepted the consulting role the next morning.

Over the following months, similar moments occurred. Each time Claire approached a decision with hesitation, the system met her with clarity. When she considered adjusting her investments, it showed long-term outcomes. When she planned a major purchase, it displayed tax-efficient timing. When she received a performance bonus, everything adjusted automatically, already accounted for.

What surprised her wasn't the accuracy.

It was the absence of effort.

She wasn't managing anything anymore. She was choosing.

One evening, Claire sat on her couch reviewing her annual financial summary. It wasn't dramatic. No alarms. No surprises. Everything matched projections made months earlier. Her taxes were already reconciled. Her compliance verified. There was nothing to prepare, nothing to fear.

And then it hit her.

The constant background tension—the low-grade anxiety she had accepted as normal—was gone.

She hadn't noticed when it left.

Claire thought back over the past year. How many decisions had she avoided before because of uncertainty? How many opportunities had she delayed because she didn't want to deal with complexity? How much mental space had been consumed by vigilance?

She realized that what she had called "responsibility" had often been fear wearing a professional mask.

The AI-managed system hadn't made her richer overnight. It hadn't eliminated work or handed her shortcuts. What it had done was remove friction. It had taken away the invisible weight she didn't know she was carrying.

With that weight gone, Claire felt lighter. More decisive. More willing to plan long-term instead of bracing short-term. Financial freedom wasn't a sudden change in numbers. It was a change in posture.

She stood taller.

Months later, Claire made a decision she had postponed for years. She negotiated a flexible role that allowed her to work fewer hours and focus on projects she truly cared about. The system showed her the impact clearly. The numbers worked. The fear didn't appear.

On the day she signed the agreement, Claire walked home slowly, aware of something new.

She wasn't escaping responsibility.

She was finally free to carry only what mattered.

The rest—the calculations, the compliance, the constant checking—had been set down gently by a system designed to hold it for her.

And in that quiet release, Claire understood the future wasn't about having more.

It was about carrying less.

Chapter 10

The End of Tax Anxiety and the Beginning of Financial Peace

The final transformation brought by AI-powered personal tax systems is not technological, legislative, or procedural. It is emotional. For centuries, taxes have been associated with anxiety, fear, and uncertainty. Even people who were responsible, organized, and financially successful carried a persistent sense of unease, rooted in the belief that something could go wrong at any time. Artificial intelligence ends this emotional cycle by eliminating the conditions that created it in the first place. When taxes are continuously managed, transparently explained, and automatically optimized, anxiety no longer has anywhere to live.

Tax anxiety has never been about paying money. It has always been about not knowing. Not knowing if income was classified correctly. Not knowing if deductions were missed. Not knowing if a mistake would surface years later with penalties attached. AI dissolves this uncertainty by replacing delayed discovery with immediate clarity. Every financial action is understood at the moment it happens. Every consequence is visible before it becomes a problem. Fear thrives in darkness, and AI floods the system with light.

This shift changes the rhythm of life. Instead of a year building toward a moment of reckoning, financial activity flows evenly. There are no peaks of stress and valleys of relief. There is only steady awareness. Taxes become predictable, manageable, and quietly resolved. This steady state allows people to relax into their financial lives rather than brace against them.

Financial peace emerges when people trust their systems. AI-powered tax platforms earn that trust through consistency. When projections match outcomes month after month, confidence replaces vigilance. People stop checking obsessively. They stop second-guessing decisions. They stop carrying the mental load of "what if." Peace is not the absence of responsibility; it is the presence of reliability.

Another critical factor in this transformation is dignity. Traditional tax systems often made people feel small, confused, or dependent. Complexity created power imbalances, where understanding was reserved for experts and institutions. AI restores dignity by making understanding accessible. When people can see and comprehend their own financial reality, they feel empowered rather than intimidated. This sense of dignity is a quiet but powerful contributor to peace.

AI also redefines success. In the past, success often brought more stress because it brought more complexity. Higher income meant higher stakes. Growth meant more risk. AI breaks this pattern by scaling effortlessly. Complexity does not increase stress because the system absorbs it. Success can expand without emotional cost. This allows people to pursue growth without fear that it will destabilize their lives.

Peace also comes from alignment. AI-managed tax systems align financial behavior with long-term goals automatically. There is no disconnect between daily decisions and future outcomes. People are not surprised by results because those results have been visible all along. This alignment creates a sense of coherence, where actions feel purposeful and outcomes feel earned.

Importantly, the end of tax anxiety does not create apathy. People do not disengage from their finances. Instead, they engage differently. Curiosity replaces fear. Planning replaces avoidance. Reflection replaces panic. AI does not numb people; it steadies them.

As this book series concludes, it becomes clear that the true promise of AI-powered personal taxes is not convenience alone. It is relief. Relief from the constant background tension that once accompanied financial responsibility. Relief from the belief that one mistake could undo years of effort. Relief from the feeling that the system was always one step ahead.

In the future shaped by intelligent systems, taxes no longer dominate attention or emotion. They simply work. And when a fundamental source of stress disappears, space opens for something better: focus, creativity, generosity, and long-term thinking. This is the real legacy of AI in personal taxation. Not just efficiency, but peace.

"The Quiet After"

Jonathan had spent most of his adult life preparing for impact.

Not in dramatic ways. Not with panic attacks or sleepless nights. But with a constant readiness, a low-grade tension that lived just beneath the surface. It showed up when he opened financial apps, when he received bonuses, when he considered investments, and especially when the calendar turned toward spring.

Tax season.

Jonathan worked as a senior operations director. He earned well, invested carefully, and prided himself on being responsible. Yet no matter how prepared he was, tax season always felt like standing in front of a door, waiting for it to open and reveal either relief or regret.

He told himself this was normal.

Responsibility, after all, was supposed to feel heavy.

Over the years, Jonathan refined his systems. Better spreadsheets. Better software. Better advisors. Each improvement helped, but none removed the underlying tension. The fear wasn't about making mistakes intentionally. It was about missing something unknowingly.

That fear followed him quietly.

When his financial ecosystem transitioned to a fully AI-managed system, Jonathan approached it cautiously. He reviewed settings. Read explanations. Verified permissions. He wanted control. The system gave it to him, but it also gave him something unexpected: silence.

At first, the silence felt wrong.

There were fewer alerts. Fewer reminders. Fewer urgent messages demanding attention. Jonathan checked the dashboard more often than necessary, expecting something to be wrong. Nothing was.

Income flowed in. Taxes adjusted automatically. Investments rebalanced with tax efficiency built in. Expenses categorized themselves. Compliance status stayed green.

Weeks passed. Then months.

The silence remained.

Jonathan noticed subtle changes in himself. He stopped bracing when checking finances. He stopped revisiting decisions late at night. He stopped replaying "what if" scenarios in his head. The system wasn't just accurate; it was consistent. Every projection it made aligned with reality. Trust grew quietly, without ceremony.

Then April arrived.

Jonathan didn't notice at first.

It wasn't until a colleague mentioned staying up late "working on taxes" that Jonathan paused. He opened his financial dashboard out of curiosity.

"Annual reconciliation complete. Filed successfully."

No fanfare. No urgency. No checklist.

He sat back in his chair, waiting for the familiar rush of relief. It didn't come.

Instead, there was something else.

Stillness. The kind of stillness that follows a storm you didn't realize had been raging for years.

Jonathan closed his laptop and stared out the window. He thought about how much mental space taxes had occupied throughout his life. How many decisions had been shaped by fear of complexity. How often he had chosen the safe path simply to avoid uncertainty.

He realized something then.

The anxiety hadn't been protecting him.

It had been exhausting him.

In the weeks that followed, Jonathan began to feel different. Lighter. Not euphoric, not careless—just steady. He made decisions without hesitation. He planned long-term without fear. He accepted a role on a nonprofit board he had declined years earlier because he didn't want to complicate his finances.

The system showed him the impact clearly.

There was no reason to say no.

One evening, Jonathan sat with his daughter as she worked on a school project about "jobs of the future." She asked him what he did.

"I make sure things run smoothly," he said.

She nodded. "So people don't worry?"

Jonathan smiled.

"Yes," he said softly. "So people don't worry."

After she went to bed, Jonathan reflected on the irony. For years, he had managed complexity for a living, yet carried unnecessary complexity in his own life. AI hadn't taken responsibility away from him. It had taken anxiety away.

And in that quiet after—the space left behind when fear finally left—Jonathan found something he hadn't expected.

Peace.

Not excitement. Not relief.

Peace.

The kind that doesn't announce itself.

The kind that simply stays.

Final Thoughts

A World Where Taxes Finally Work for You

The journey through this book, and through the entire AI Personal Tax Optimization series, has been a journey away from fear and toward clarity. For decades, personal taxation has been treated as an unavoidable burden—something endured rather than understood, something survived rather than integrated into life. What artificial intelligence ultimately delivers is not merely efficiency, but resolution. It resolves the tension between earning and owing, between growth and complexity, between responsibility and peace of mind.

The most important realization is this: taxes were never meant to dominate mental space. They became overwhelming only because systems were built for a different era—an era of paper, delays, human error, and fragmented information. AI corrects that mismatch. It aligns taxation with the way modern life already works: digitally, continuously, and in real time. When systems reflect reality, friction disappears.

Throughout this book, a clear pattern has emerged. Stress does not come from paying taxes; it comes from uncertainty. Anxiety does not come from responsibility; it comes from delayed feedback. Fear does not come from compliance; it comes from complexity without explanation. Artificial intelligence removes these conditions entirely. By making tax awareness continuous, compliance automatic, and optimization proactive, AI closes the gap where anxiety once lived.

What makes this transformation profound is that it scales with life. As income grows, complexity grows—but stress does not. As investments expand, reporting obligations increase—but fear does not. As opportunities multiply, decision-making becomes easier—not harder. AI absorbs complexity at the same rate life generates it, creating a stable emotional and financial environment even as circumstances evolve.

This is why the future described in this book feels quieter than expected. There are no dramatic breakthroughs to manage, no heroic efforts required from individuals. The change happens in the background. Taxes fade from attention not because they are ignored, but because they are handled correctly. The absence of stress is not accidental; it is engineered.

The most meaningful outcome of AI-powered personal taxation is not lower bills, faster filing, or smarter planning—though all of those matter. The true outcome is space. Mental space. Emotional space. Strategic space. When taxes stop consuming attention, people gain room to think long-term, to act intentionally, and to live with confidence rather than caution.

This is the final promise of AI in personal taxes: not a system that demands trust, but one that earns it through consistency, transparency, and reliability. Not a system that replaces human responsibility, but one that supports it quietly and continuously. Not a system that changes who you are, but one that removes what never needed to be carried in the first place.

As you close this book, the future it describes is no longer theoretical. It is already forming. The only real decision left is whether to resist the quiet transformation or step into it willingly. Those who do will not feel like they have gained something extraordinary. They will feel something far more valuable.

They will feel at peace.

www.ingramcontent.com/pod-product-compliance
Lightning Source LLC
LaVergne TN
LVHW022020200926
848481LV00007B/2456